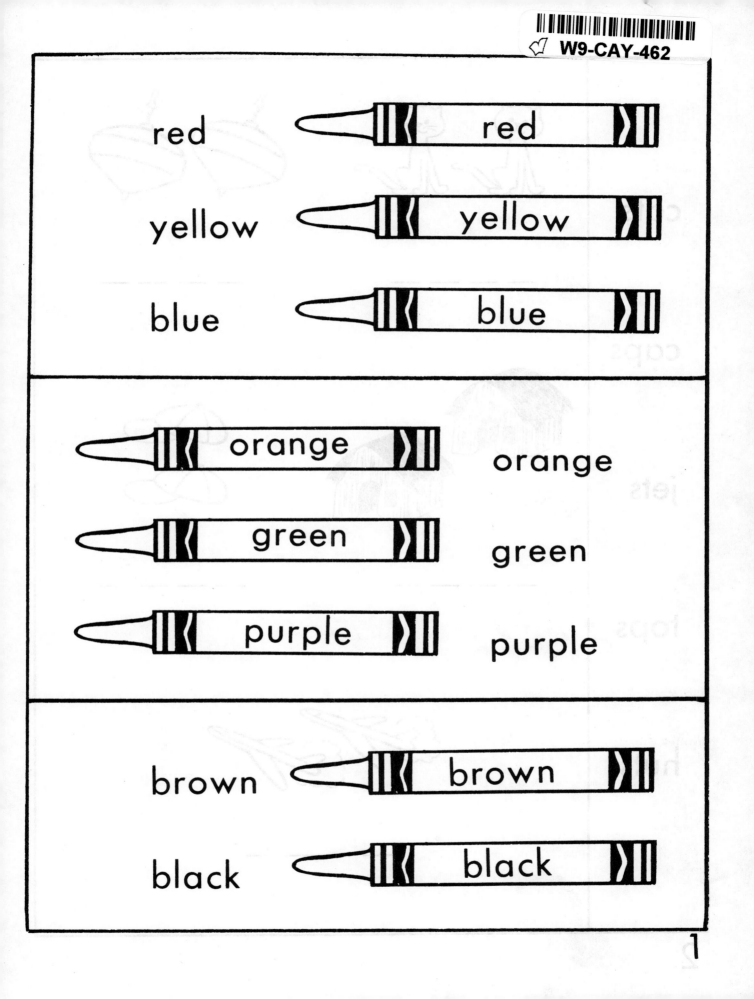

red    red

yellow    yellow

blue    blue

orange    orange

green    green

purple    purple

brown    brown

black    black

cats

caps

jets

tops

huts

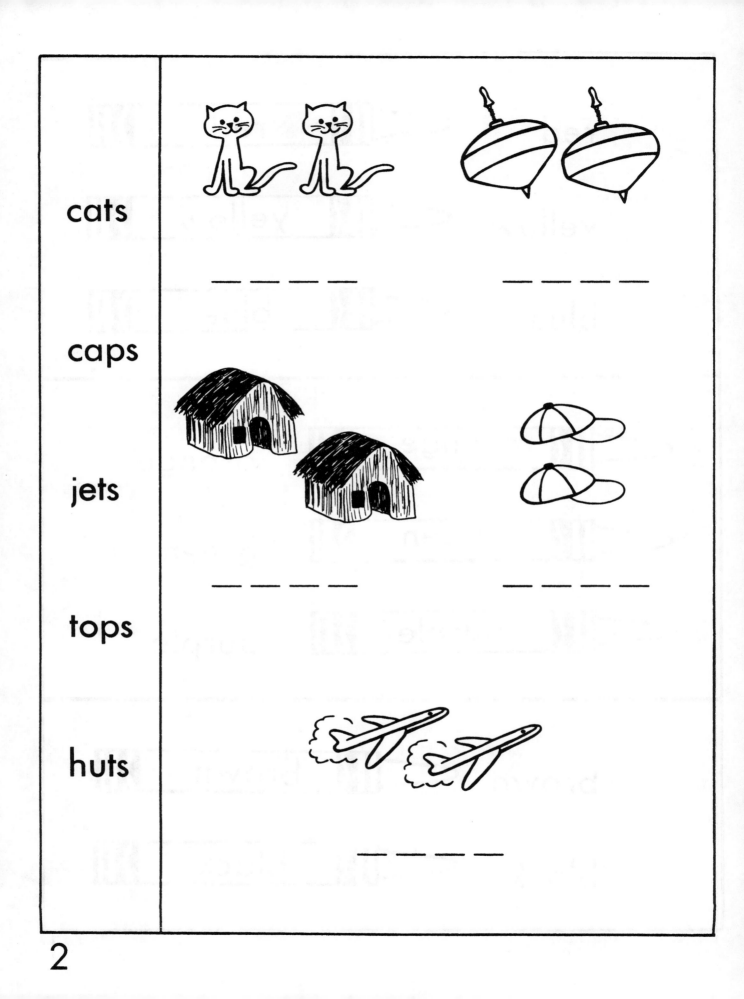

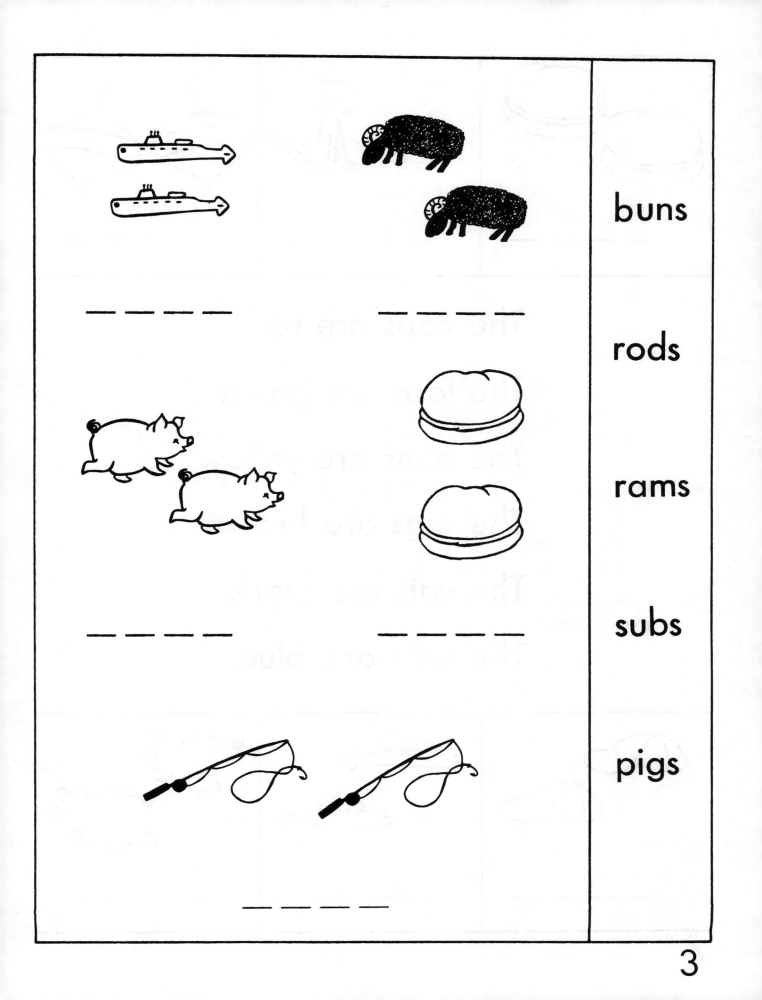

buns

rods

rams

subs

pigs

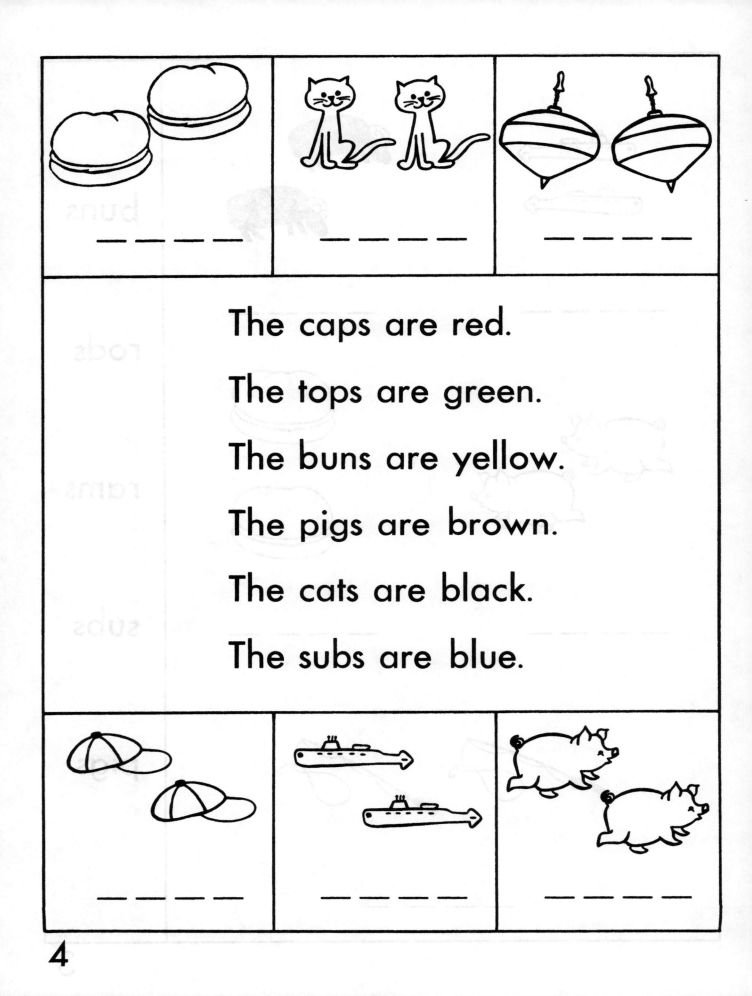

The caps are red.

The tops are green.

The buns are yellow.

The pigs are brown.

The cats are black.

The subs are blue.

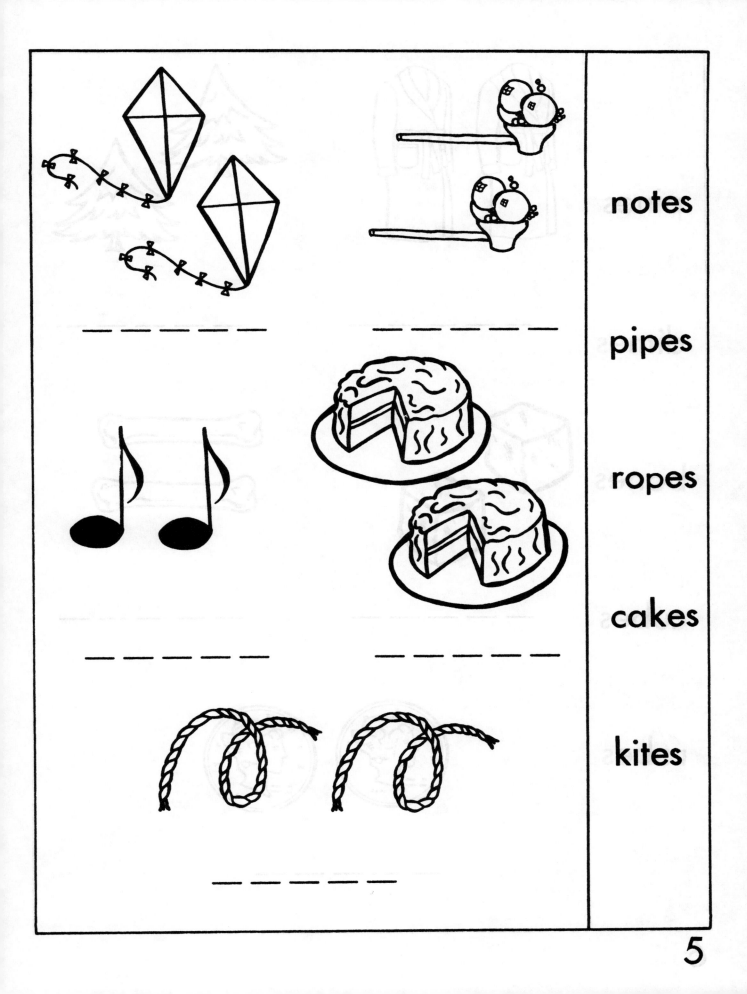

notes

pipes

ropes

cakes

kites

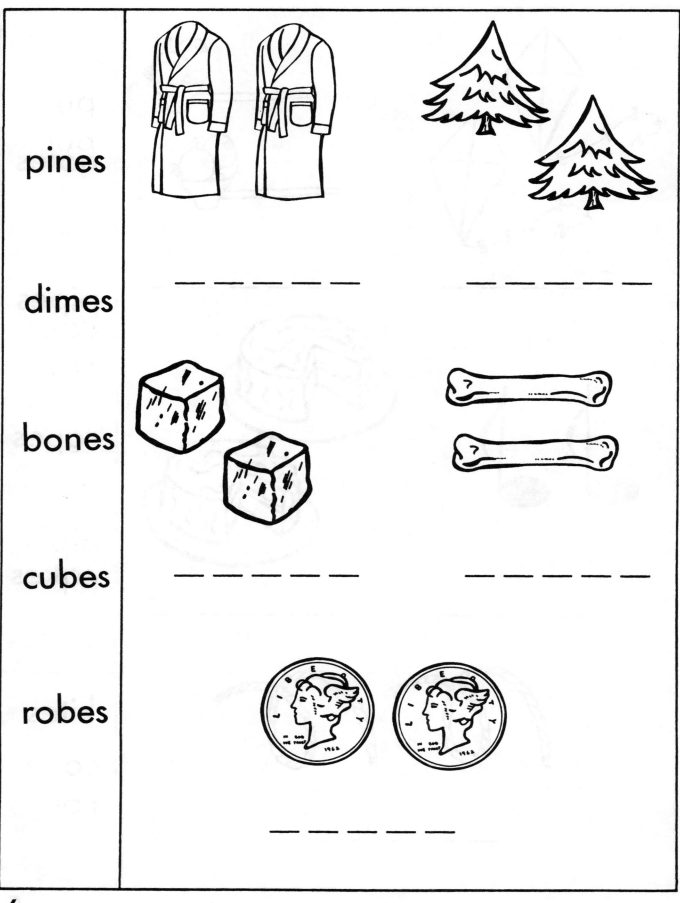

pines

dimes

- - - - - - -          - - - - - - -

bones

cubes

- - - - - - -          - - - - - - -

robes

- - - - - - -

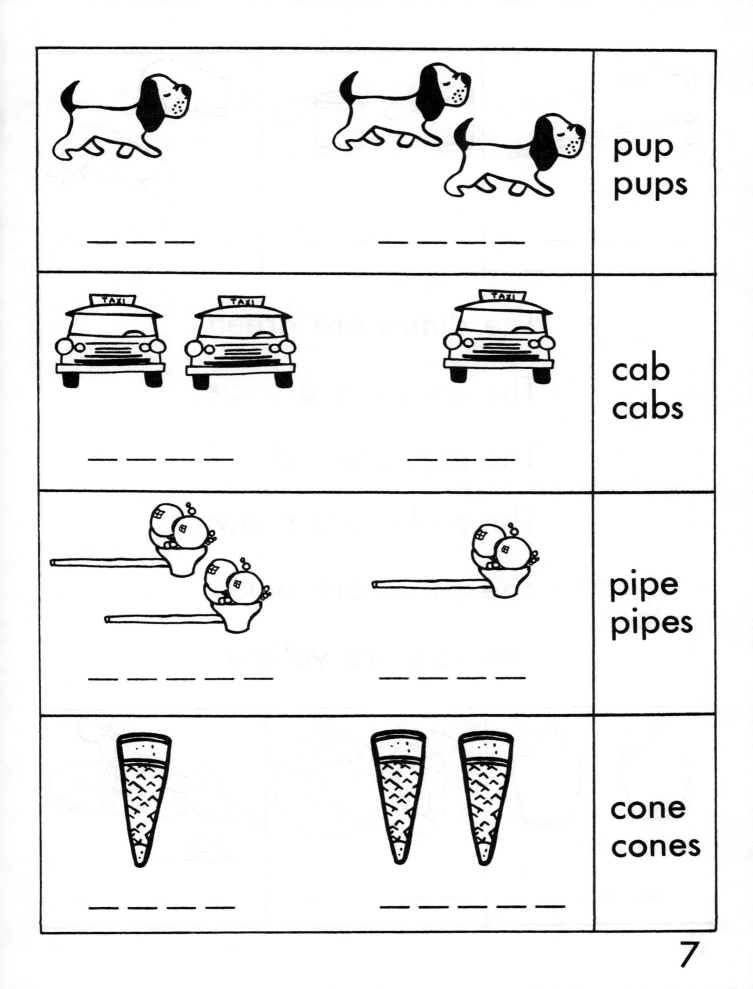

pup
pups

_ _ _ _       _ _ _ _

cab
cabs

_ _ _ _ _       _ _ _ _

pipe
pipes

_ _ _ _ _ _       _ _ _ _ _

cone
cones

_ _ _ _ _       _ _ _ _ _ _

7

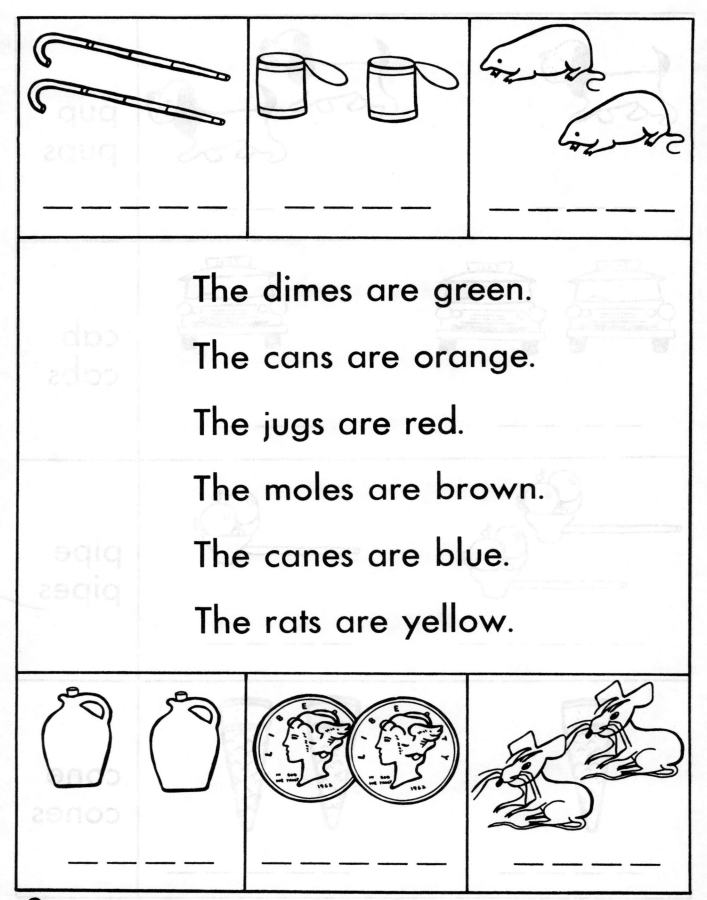

The dimes are green.

The cans are orange.

The jugs are red.

The moles are brown.

The canes are blue.

The rats are yellow.

boats

beaks

jeeps

goats

beets

teams

seals

nails

bees

oars

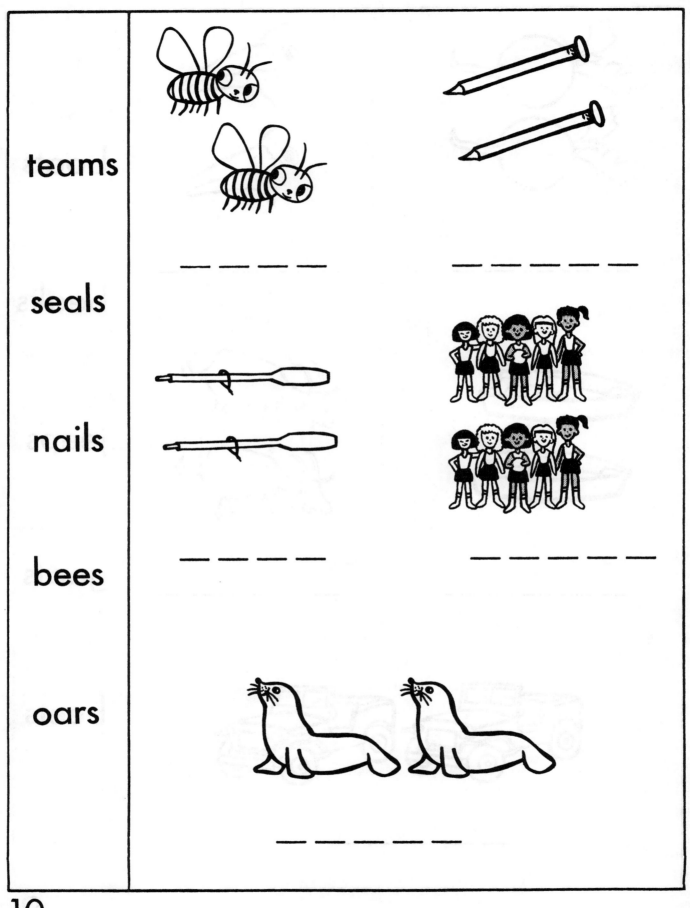

| | | goats | The |
| --- | --- | gates | are |
| | | the | on |

· · · · · · · · · · · · · · · · · · · · · · · · · · · · · · · · · · · · · · · · · · · · · · · · · · · · · · · · · · · · · · · · · · · · · · · · · · · · · · · · · · · · · · · · · · · · · · · · · · · · · · · · · · · · · · · · · · · · · · · · · · · · · · · · · · · · · · · · · · · · · · · · · · · · · · · · · · · · · · · · · · · · · · · · · · · · · · · · · · · · · · · · · · · · · · · · · · · · · · · · · · · · · · · · · · · · · · · · · · · · · · · · · · · · · · · · · · · · · · · · · · · · · · · · · · · · · · · · · · · ·

· · · · · · · · · · · · · · · · · · · · · · · · · · · · · · · · · · · · · · · · · · · · · · · · · · · · · · · · · · · · · · · · · · · · · · · · · · · · · · · · · · · · · · · · · · · · · · · · · · · · · · · · · · · · · · · · · · · · · · · · · · · · · · · · · · · · · · · · · · · · · · · · · · · · · · · · · · · · · · · · · · · · · · · · · · · · · · · · · · · · · · · · · · · · · · · · · · · · · · · · · · · · · · · · · · · · · · · · · · · · · · · · · · · · · · · · · · · · · · · · · · · · · · · · · · · · · · · · · · · · ·

| | | The | on |
| --- | --- | beads | are |
| | | bees | the |

· · · · · · · · · · · · · · · · · · · · · · · · · · · · · · · · · · · · · · · · · · · · · · · · · · · · · · · · · · · · · · · · · · · · · · · · · · · · · · · · · · · · · · · · · · · · · · · · · · · · · · · · · · · · · · · · · · · · · · · · · · · · · · · · · · · · · · · · · · · · · · · · · · · · · · · · · · · · · · · · · · · · · · · · · · · · · · · · · · · · · · · · · · · · · · · · · · · · · · · · · · · · · · · · · · · · · · · · · · · · · · · · · · · · · · · · · · · · · · · · · · · · · · · · · · · · · · · · · · · · ·

· · · · · · · · · · · · · · · · · · · · · · · · · · · · · · · · · · · · · · · · · · · · · · · · · · · · · · · · · · · · · · · · · · · · · · · · · · · · · · · · · · · · · · · · · · · · · · · · · · · · · · · · · · · · · · · · · · · · · · · · · · · · · · · · · · · · · · · · · · · · · · · · · · · · · · · · · · · · · · · · · · · · · · · · · · · · · · · · · · · · · · · · · · · · · · · · · · · · · · · · · · · · · · · · · · · · · · · · · · · · · · · · · · · · · · · · · · · · · · · · · · · · · · · · · · · · · · · · · · · · ·

11

The cubs are brown.

The ties are blue.

The pails are purple.

The files are yellow.

The pops are orange.

The bugs are green.

12

steps

stop

stone

store

stove

street

| | | |
|---|---|---|
| stone<br>store | | |
| | _ _ _ _ _ _ _ | _ _ _ _ _ _ _ |
| steps<br>stop | | |
| | _ _ _ _ _ _ _ | _ _ _ _ _ _ _ |
| stone<br>stove | | |
| | _ _ _ _ _ _ _ | _ _ _ _ _ _ _ |
| steps<br>street | | |
| | _ _ _ _ _ _ _ | _ _ _ _ _ _ _ |

14

sled

slip

slide

slate

plum

plug

plane

plate

____ ____ ____ ____

The stone is black.

The store is green.

The slide is yellow.

The sled is red.

The plane is blue.

The plum is purple.

____ ____ ____ ____

clam

clap

clip

class

flag

flat

globe

blue

- - - - - -

- - - - - -

- - - - - -

- - - - - -

- - - - - -

- - - - - -

17

| top<br>stop | _ _ _ _ | _ _ _ |
| lip<br>clip | _ _ _ _ | _ _ _ _ |
| late<br>plate<br>slate | _ _ _ _ _ | _ _ _ _ _ |

18

drip

drop

drag

drum

drive

frog

The frog is green.

The clam is brown.

The drop is blue.

The clip is yellow.

The drum is red.

The globe is blue.

20

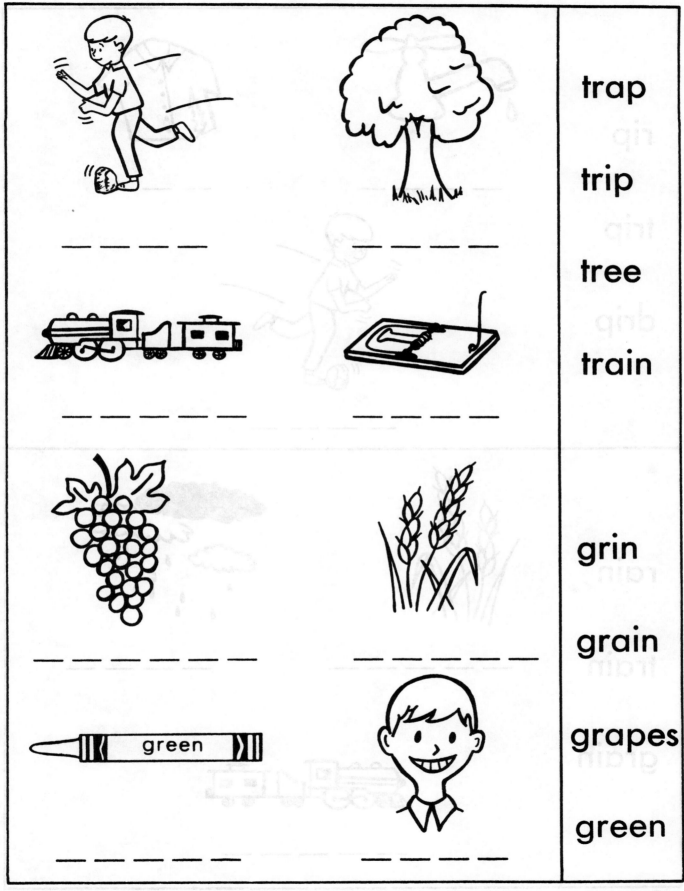

trap

trip

tree

train

grin

grain

grapes

green

green

21

rip

trip

drip

rain

train

grain

crib

crab

creek

_ _ _ _ _          _ _ _ _ _

_ _ _ _ _

braids

bride

_ _ _ _ _          _ _ _ _ _

_ _ _ _     _ _ _ _ _     _ _ _ _ _

The trap is red.

The plane is orange.

The plug is brown.

The stove is yellow.

The crab is brown.

The train is green.

_ _ _ _     _ _ _ _ _     _ _ _ _

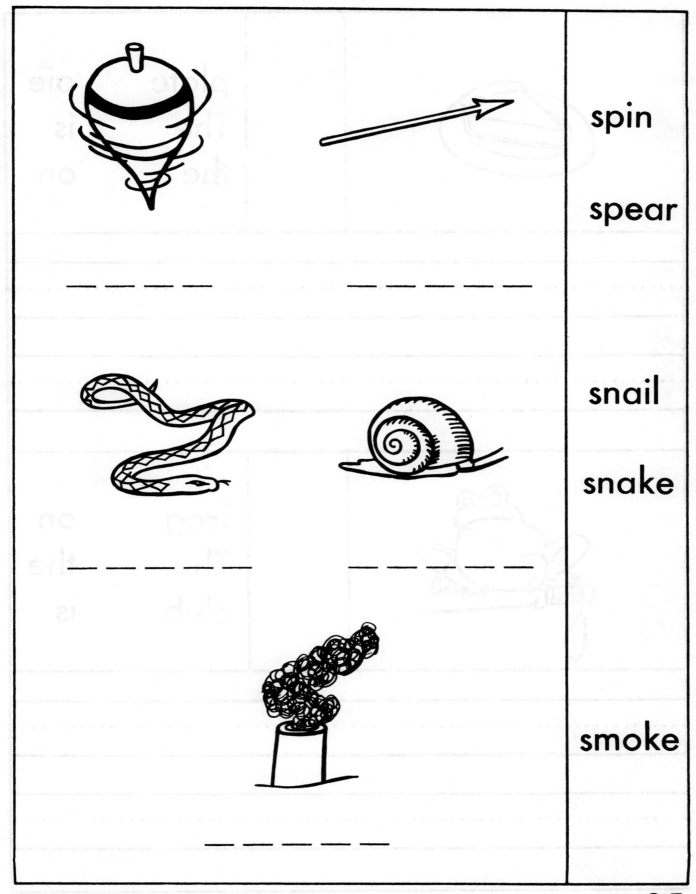

spin

spear

_ _ _ _ _ _ _ _ _ _ _ _ _ _

snail

snake

_ _ _ _ _ _ _ _ _ _ _ _ _ _

smoke

_ _ _ _ _

| | | plate      pie |
| --- | --- | --- |
| | | The       is |
| | | the       on |

| | | frog      on |
| --- | --- | --- |
| | | The     the |
| | | club     is |

sweep

swim

twins

scale

skate

27

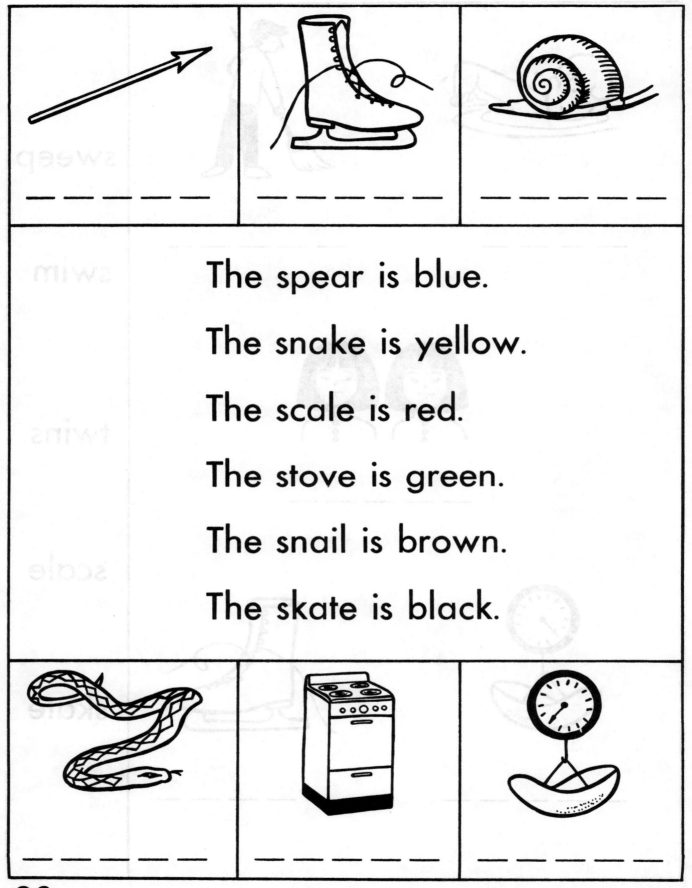

The spear is blue.

The snake is yellow.

The scale is red.

The stove is green.

The snail is brown.

The skate is black.

28

| The | is |
|-----|-----|
| nail | the |
| snail | on |

| steps | is |
|-------|-----|
| train | on |
| the | The |

| ride bride | | |
|---|---|---|
| nail snail | | |
| rain train | | |
| pin spin | | |

— — — — —     — — — —

| | Yes | No |
|---|---|---|
| Is the flag on the snail? | _____ | |
| Is the flag on the plate? | _____ | |
| Is the snake on the snail? | _____ | |
| Is the frog on the plate? | _____ | |
| Is the snake on the steps? | _____ | |
| Is the frog on the steps? | _____ | |

The snail is brown.
The steps are red.
The plate is purple.
The frog is green.
The snake is yellow.
The flag is blue.

slide
slip
_____

grapes
globe
_____

sweep
swim
_____

plane
plate
_____

bride
braids
_____

grin
green
_____

twins
train
_____

store
stove
_____

Now you can read storybooks 1-3 listed on the back cover.

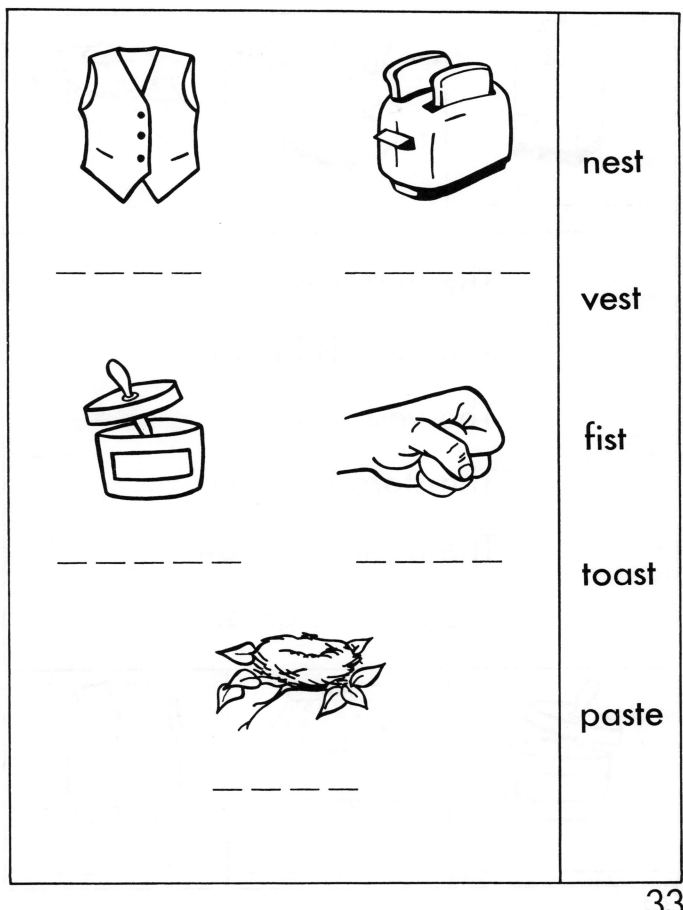

nest

vest

fist

toast

paste

The nest is brown.

The toast is brown.

The vest is red.

The store is green.

The paste is yellow.

The stove is green.

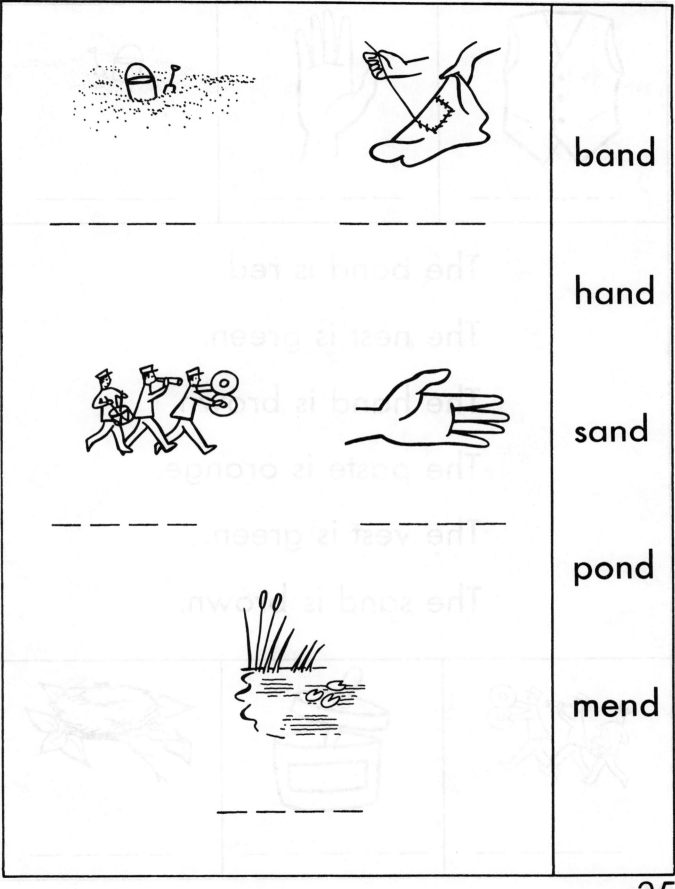

band

hand

sand

pond

mend

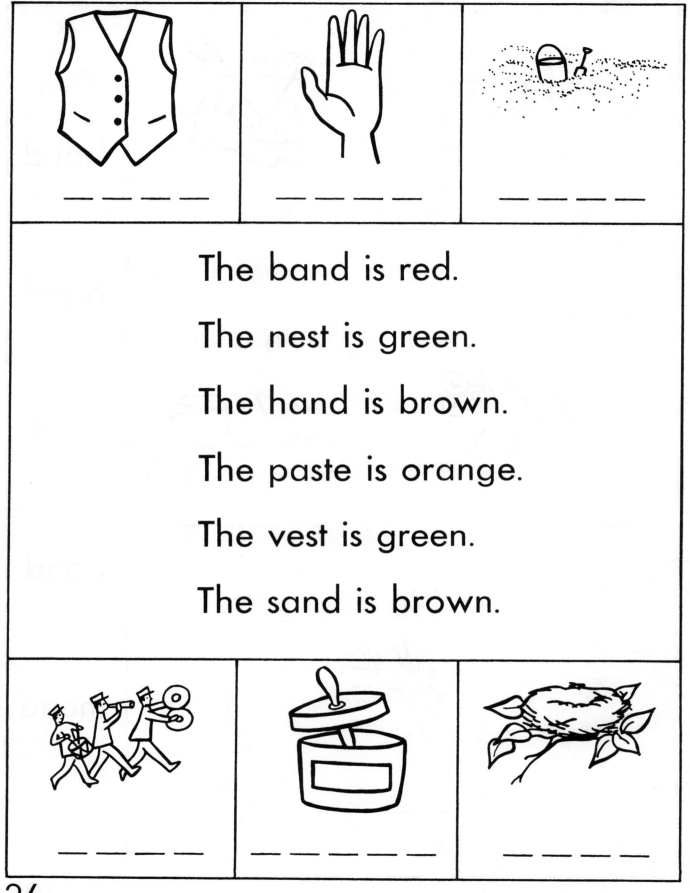

The band is red.

The nest is green.

The hand is brown.

The paste is orange.

The vest is green.

The sand is brown.

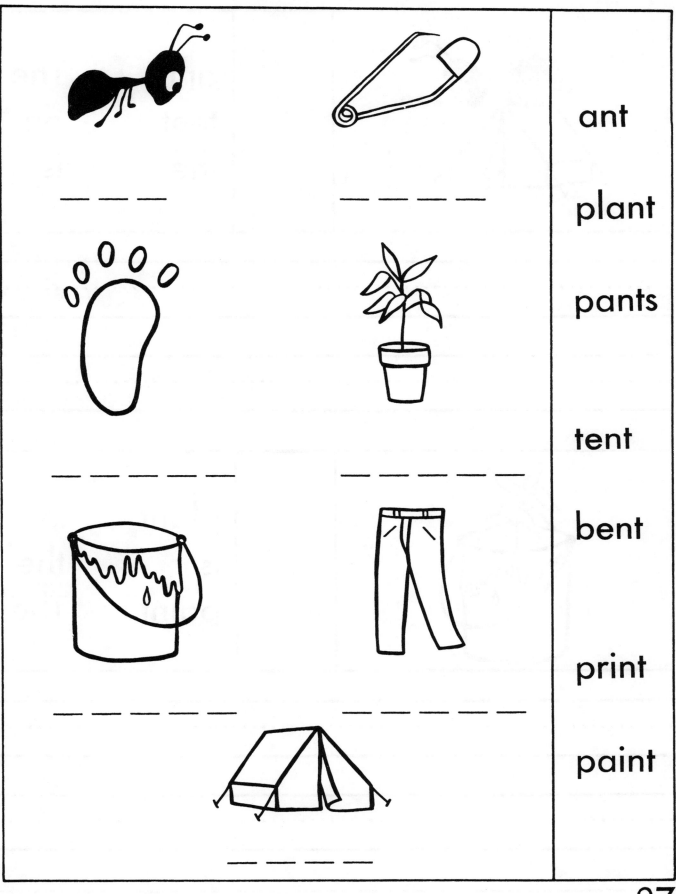

ant

plant

pants

tent

bent

print

paint

37

| | | ant | The |
| | | tent | on |
| | | the | is |

| | | plant | in |
| | | is | the |
| | | paint | The |

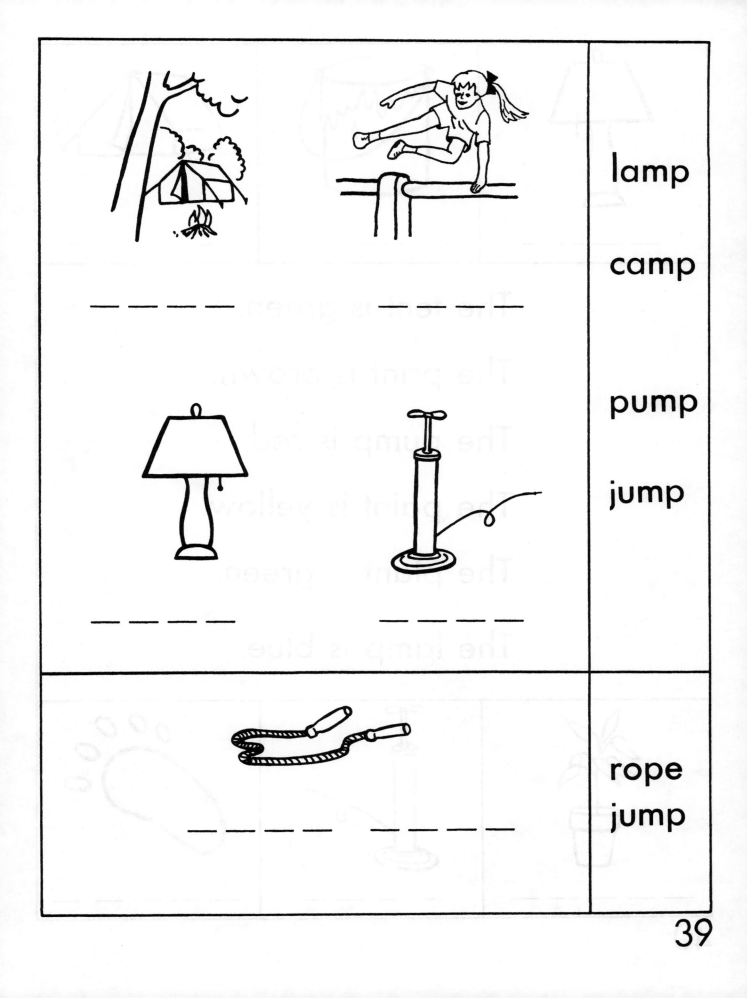

lamp

camp

_ _ _ _ _ _

pump

jump

_ _ _ _ _          _ _ _ _ _

rope

jump

_ _ _ _ _ _ _ _

The tent is green.

The print is brown.

The pump is red.

The paint is yellow.

The plant is green.

The lamp is blue.

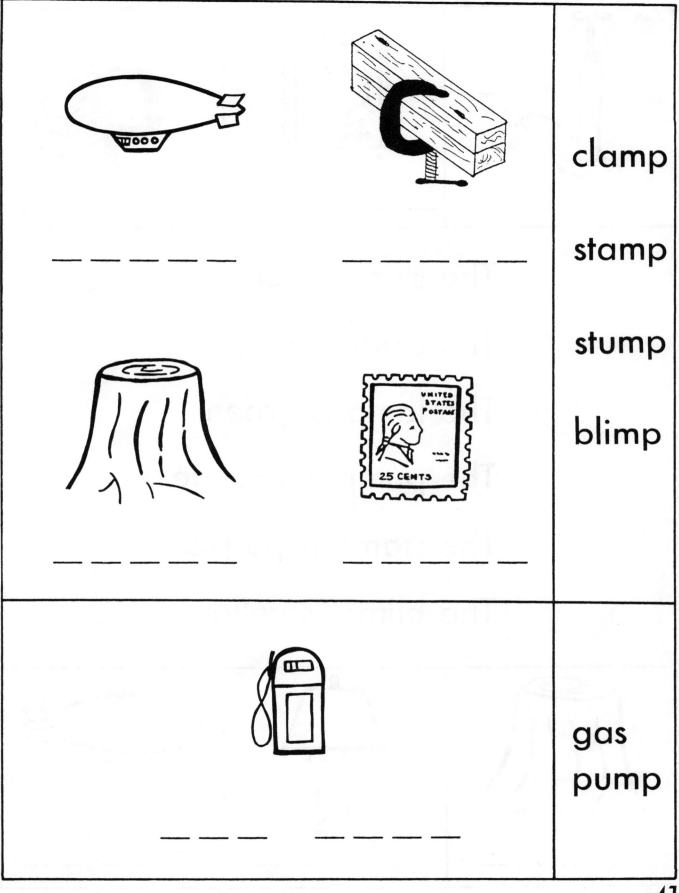

clamp

stamp

stump

blimp

_ _ _ _ _ _ _

_ _ _ _ _ _ _

_ _ _ _ _ _ _

_ _ _ _ _ _ _

gas
pump

_ _ _ _ _ _ _

The stump is brown.

The clamp is blue.

The lamp is green.

The pump is orange.

The stamp is purple.

The blimp is yellow.

sift

gift

raft

_ _ _ _

_ _ _ _

desk

mask

_ _ _ _          _ _ _ _

| | | The | the |
| --- | --- | rat | in |
| | | raft | is |

......................................................

......................................................

| | | goat | on |
| --- | --- | gift | is |
| | | the | The |

......................................................

......................................................

44

melt

belt

elf

milk

bulb

_ _ _ _

45

The bulb is yellow.

The milk is red.

The elf is green.

The belt is blue.

The raft is brown.

The mask is black.

|  | Yes | No |
|---|---|---|
| Is the ant on the desk? | _____ |  |
| Is the clamp on the desk? | _____ |  |
| Is the clamp on the raft? | _____ |  |
| Is the elf on the ant? | _____ |  |
| Is the hand on the raft? | _____ |  |
| Is the elf on the hand? | _____ |  |

The hand is brown.
The desk is red.
The clamp is blue.
The ant is black.
The elf is green.
The raft is yellow.

| | |
|---|---|
| tramp<br>train | toast<br>tent |
| milk<br>mask | paint<br>plant |
| stamp<br>sand | belt<br>bulb |
| pond<br>pump | pants<br>paste |

48

Now you can read storybooks 4-6 listed on the back cover.

boat

sail

fire

man

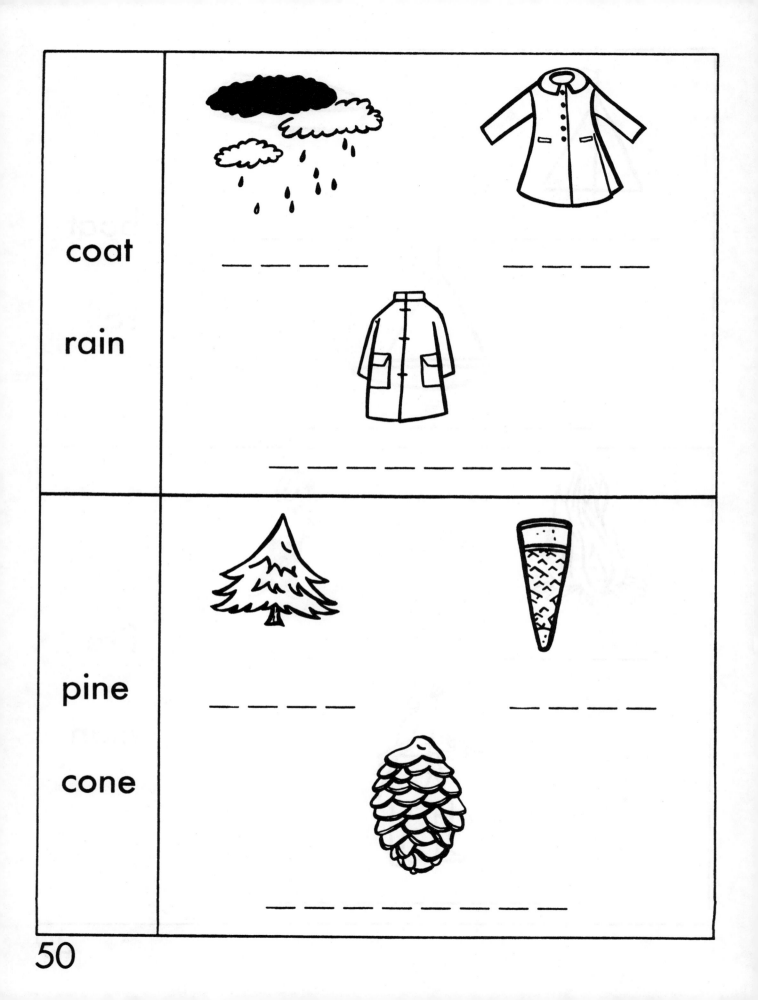

coat

rain

_ _ _ _ _ _

_ _ _ _ _ _

pine

cone

_ _ _ _ _ _

_ _ _ _ _ _

50

book

note

cake

cup

tea

pot

_ _ _          _ _ _

_ _ _ _ _ _

man

mail

_ _ _ _          _ _ _

_ _ _ _ _ _

The teapot is green.

The raincoat is yellow.

The pinecone is brown.

The sailboat is red.

| is | the |
|---|---|
| The | elf |
| sailboat | on |

| mailman | in |
|---|---|
| raft | the |
| is | The |

kitten

mitten

rabbit

puppet

button

napkin

cactus

magnet

blanket

basket

| | | cactus    is |
| | | The    cat |
| | | on    the |

..............................................................................

..............................................................................

| | | puppet    pup |
| | | is    The |
| | | on    the |

..............................................................................

..............................................................................

The kitten is yellow.

The napkin is blue.

The cactus is green.

The rabbit is brown.

The mitten is purple.

The puppet is red.

Now you can read the storybook *Mittens*.

hill

quill

spill

drill

mill

grill

fell

sell

bell

well

skull

gull

doll

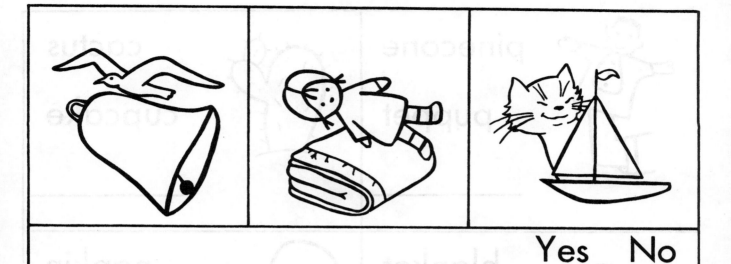

| | Yes | No |
|---|---|---|
| Is the kitten on the sailboat? | _____ | |
| Is the gull on the blanket? | _____ | |
| Is the doll on the sailboat? | _____ | |
| Is the gull on the bell? | _____ | |
| Is the kitten on the bell? | _____ | |
| Is the doll on the blanket? | _____ | |

The doll is red.
The blanket is green.
The sailboat is blue.
The gull is brown.
The kitten is yellow.
The bell is orange.

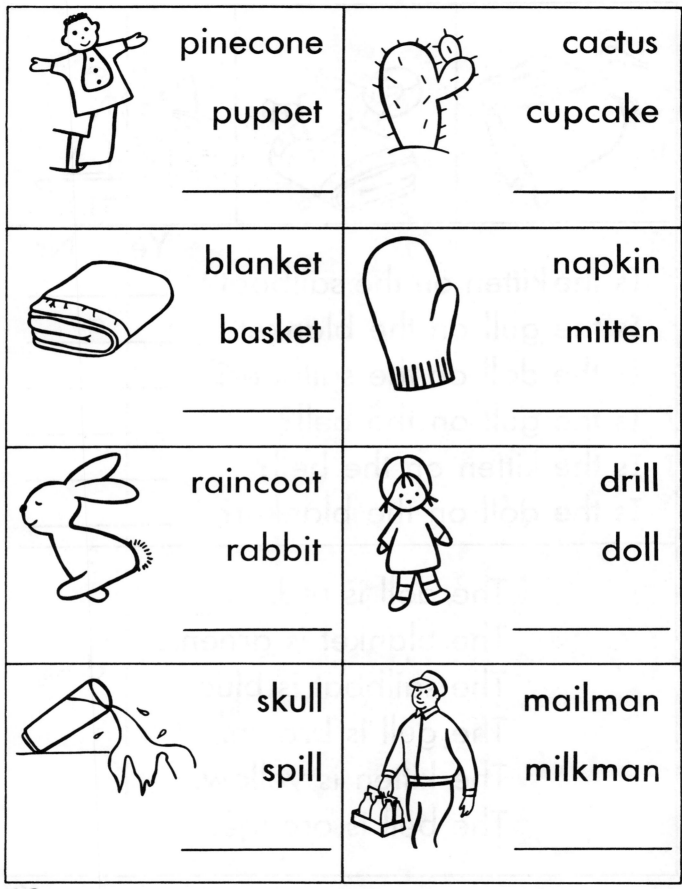

pinecone

puppet

_____

cactus

cupcake

_____

blanket

basket

_____

napkin

mitten

_____

raincoat

rabbit

_____

drill

doll

_____

skull

spill

_____

mailman

milkman

_____

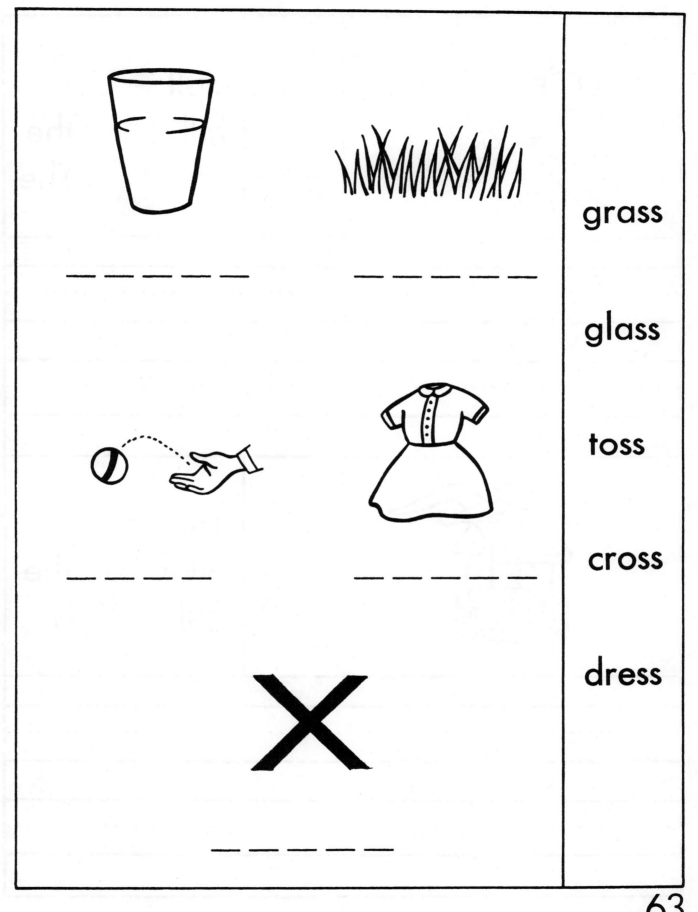

grass

glass

toss

cross

dress

| | | doll         is |
| | | hill     the |
| | | on       The |

····································································

····································································

| | | The     on |
| | | well   the |
| | | gull    is |

····································································

····································································

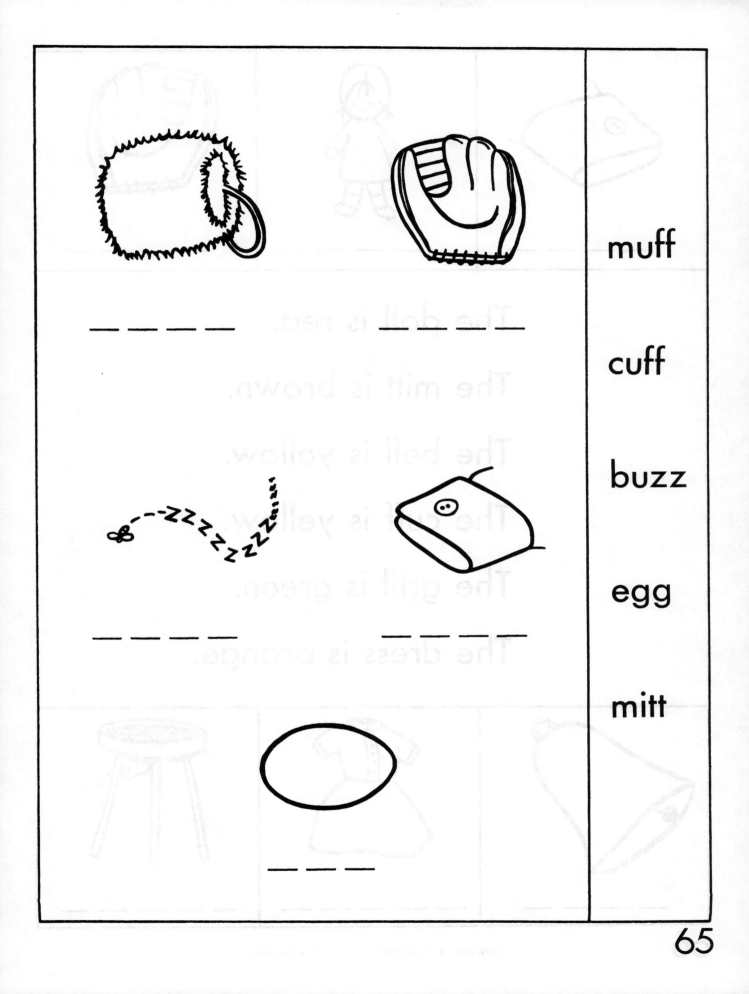

muff

cuff

buzz

egg

mitt

_ _ _ _ _ _

_ _ _ _ _ _

_ _ _ _

___ ___ ___

___ ___ ___

___ ___ ___

The doll is red.

The mitt is brown.

The bell is yellow.

The cuff is yellow.

The grill is green.

The dress is orange.

___ ___ ___

___ ___ ___

___ ___ ___

Now you can read the storybook *The Sea Gull.*

lock

clock

block

sock

dock

duck

truck

67

| | | lock    is<br>The    on<br>block    the |
| --- | --- | --- |

| | | truck    The<br>is      the<br>duck    on |
| --- | --- | --- |

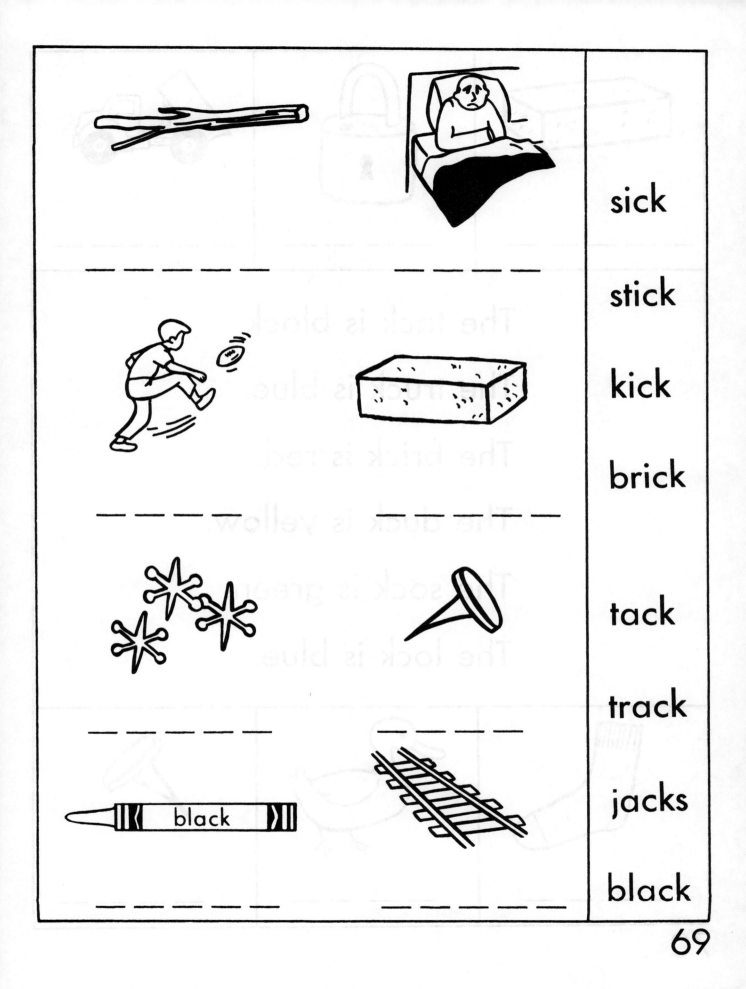

sick

stick

kick

brick

tack

track

jacks

black

_ _ _ _ _     _ _ _ _     _ _ _ _ _

The tack is black.

The truck is blue.

The brick is red.

The duck is yellow.

The sock is green.

The lock is blue.

_ _ _ _     _ _ _ _     _ _ _ _

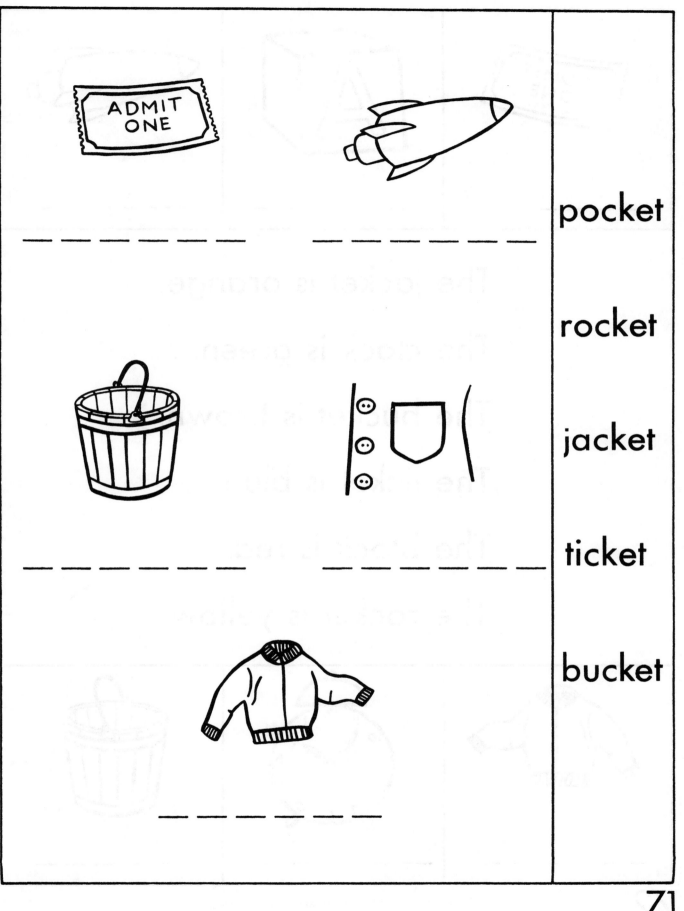

pocket

rocket

jacket

ticket

bucket

_ _ _ _ _ _ | _ _ _ _ _ | _ _ _ _ _ _

The jacket is orange.

The clock is green.

The bucket is brown.

The ticket is blue.

The block is red.

The rocket is yellow.

_ _ _ _ _ _ | _ _ _ _ _ | _ _ _ _ _ _

72

Now you can read the storybook *The Lost Duck.*

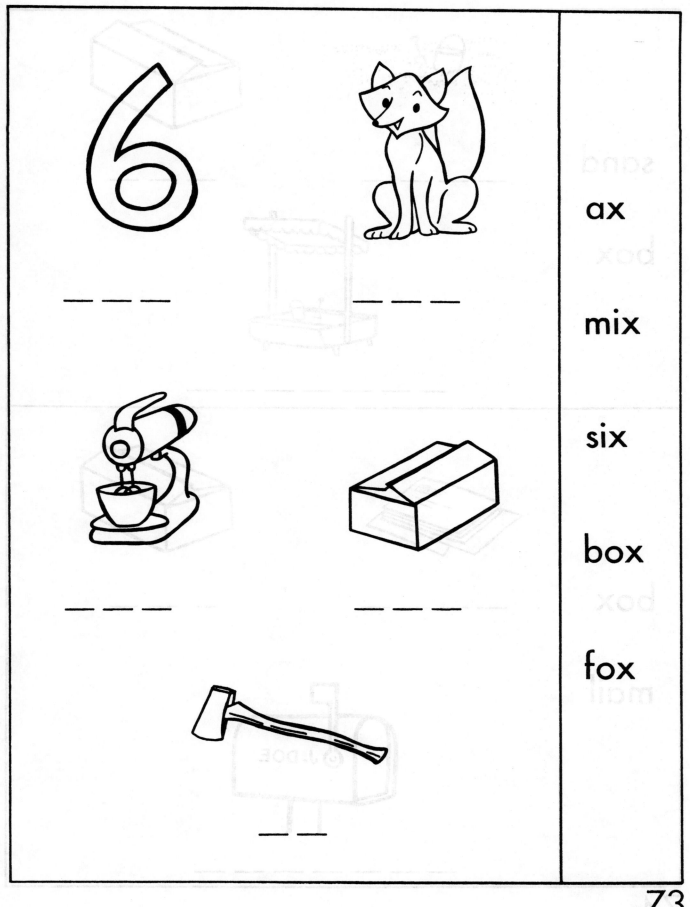

6

ax

mix

six

box

fox

_ _ _ _     _ _ _ _

_ _ _ _     _ _ _ _

_ _ _

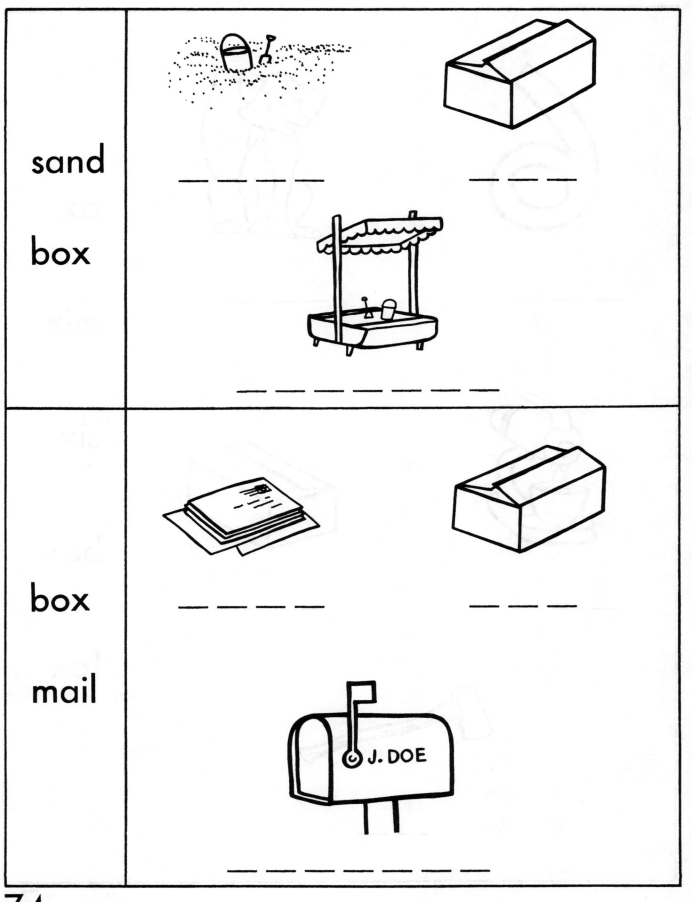

sand

box

\_ \_ \_ \_ \_ \_ \_      \_ \_ \_ \_ \_

\_ \_ \_ \_ \_ \_ \_ \_ \_

box

mail

\_ \_ \_ \_ \_ \_ \_      \_ \_ \_ \_ \_

\_ \_ \_ \_ \_ \_ \_ \_ \_

| | | fox box |
| | | is in |
| | | The the |

| | | mailbox in |
| | | ax is |
| | | the The |

mend

trip

clap

jump

drive

toss

kick

swim

_ _ _ _

_ _ _ _

_ _ _ _

_ _ _ _

_ _ _ _

_ _ _ _

_ _ _ _

_ _ _ _

Yes   No

Is the duck in the box? _____

Is the ant on the train? _____

Is the ant in the basket? _____

Is the duck in the basket? _____

Is the kitten on the train? _____

Is the kitten in the box? _____

The box is brown.
The kitten is orange.
The duck is yellow.
The ant is black.
The basket is green.
The train is red.

block
black
_____

duck
drop
_____

truck
train
_____

grass
grill
_____

jacket
jacks
_____

drum
dress
_____

stick
sick
_____

ticket
tack
_____

78

_ _ _ _ _ _ _

_ _ _ _ _ _ _

_ _ _ _ _ _ _

_ _ _ _ _ _ _

_ _ _ _ _ _ _

_ _ _ _ _ _ _

_ _ _ _ _ _ _

_ _ _ _ _ _ _

_ _ _ _ _ _ _